Empowered by Grace

What You Need To Start Living An Outstanding Life Today

EMPOWERED BY GRACE
What You Need To Start Living An Outstanding Life Today

ISBN-13: 978-0978159542
© 2015 by Ade & Olu Sobanjo
All rights reserved.

Published by Afropages
Kingston, Ontario, Canada.

Printed in USA.

Dedication

To everyone that God has used to support us in this work of ministry so far. This includes but not limited to every member of the Olowosoyo and Olubanjo (Sobanjo) families, Members of Overcomers Assembly Canada and Overcomers Fellowship International, Nigeria; friends all over the world that continue to support us in many ways, readers and clients on our blogs.

Thanks for all your support, may God continue to bless you.

Empowered by Grace

What you need to start living an outstanding life today.

"So let us come boldly to the throne of our gracious God. There we will receive his mercy, and we will find grace to help us when we need it most." (Hebrews 4: 16 ESV)

Ade and Olu Sobanjo

Overcomers International

www.iAmAnOvercomer.org

Contents

Acknowledgements

How to get the most from this study

Introduction

1.	The Original Plan	1
2.	Image and likeness	9
3.	The Void and the pseudo power	19
4.	Grace at Calvary and beyond	35
5.	Your New Identity	45
	by Ade Sobanjo	
6.	Getting out of the rot	63
7.	Empowered for His Glory	75
	by Ade Sobanjo	

Other tools   83

About the authors

Acknowledgements

Writing a book together is a thing we had thought about before but never really planned it out. This came in a rush. I (Olu) had planned to get a book ready for our annual ladies conference (in Montreal, Canada) and I was running out of time. Then one day it hit me: "Aha! I can share the responsibilities with Ade!". Being my best friend and pastor, Ade is one of my best and effective earthly teachers; he has worked hand in hand with the Holy Spirit to teach me many things I now know. So he didn't have a choice but to say yes. And the result is what you are holding today.

The process was made easier with the help of people like:

Ade Sobanjo, my darling husband, who gracefully accepted the assignment of adding necessary content to this book that is in your hands today.

Andrea Flutsch, my accountability support and friend, who helped to deliver a reminder every week for me to work on the book. This support and accountability has helped again this second time.

Dr Bola Olubanjo, my dear sister, who is always ready to edit for us when she has ample time and when we take over the little time she has left to rest after a busy medical practice. This time she was even the one asking about the progress of the book to speed up the action.

Rose Wangeci Ntone, Ine Olude and Cynthia Egbunonu (my dear friends and Executive Directors of our annual ladies Conference) that made sure I did not quit the goal to produce a book this year but insisted the book be written.

Demi and Dami, our wonderful sons, who are gradually growing into fine young men and are learning to love God as they grow as we serve God togeth as a family. Thanks for your understanding again this time. You guys know what book is next, right?

Bate Atabong, who worked hard to make sure the book was available at the conference.

You, for choosing to go through the following pages with an open mind and allow God to transform you with His words.

God bless you all!

How to Get The Most From This Material

Empowered by Grace is designed for people that are tired of their inability to thrive in life and in their walk with God, those who are ready to move to the next level. It has seven easy to read chapters; you may choose to either go through it on your day off or over the next seven weeks, just don't rush through.

You may choose to read this in a group, for example you may ask a close friend to join you as you read. Group work helps as you use the insight from another individual in your own personal growth. However, do not neglect any prompting by the Holy Spirit to spend some time alone in prayer. Personal reflections are vital to growth (this is when you close the book and meditate and possibly write down what is coming to your mind), they give you the opportunity to dig deep and let yourself go as high or as deep as God will take you.

The story is told of a woman desperately in need of help and a man from her church that went to her home with some money to give to her. He got there and knocked on the door several times but received no response. He concluded she was not at home so he left. The next day he met her at church and told her that he had remembered her need: "I came by to your home yesterday and knocked several times, and I supposed you were away because I didn't get any response". "About what time was that?" "It was about noon." "Oh dear", she said, "I heard you, sir, and I am so sorry I did not answer; I actually thought it was the man calling for the rent." [1]

Many times we miss the answers to our prayers. We get so close and then we give up. The same thing we have been hoping for and dreaming to see comes knocking and we ignore it or walk away.

You can rest assured that this book is not going to do the work for you. Throughout the book we will recommend things for you to think on and pray about. However, you will need to step out in faith and act.

The one message we are trusting that the Holy Spirit reveals to you through this book is that you have been empowered by God's grace and Christ in you is all you need. This empowerment is not only for salvation as most people already accepted, but for an outstanding life.

Note that this book is not to make you feel bad about your life. Its purpose is to get you to see what you already have access to through Christ. If ever you start feeling shame, fear, guilt, or any other such feelings, you need to retrace your thoughts, clear your mind of every negative thought, and then embrace whom God made you to be.

May God help you!

---

[1] The story of the lady was adapted from "All of Grace" by C. H Spurgeon. On the Olive Tree Bible Study App.

Introduction

Are you tired of trying to fit in? Are you fed up of wearing different faces at different places? Do you feel paralyzed by your past mistakes? Have you paid high dues in the school of failure? Are you bound by fear of what may or may not happen if you try? Are you tired of making efforts to measure up to an expectation? Are you tired of the competition to prove who you really are? Do you dread living an insignificant life? Are you tired of playing it safe and wishing to be set free to run? If you answered yes to any of these questions it may be that you are ready to accept the empowerment that is from God to you; to dig deep and find true satisfaction in all areas of your life in Christ alone.

Welcome to Empowered by Grace, a tool that will help you to start living an outstanding life today. The aim of writing this book is to guide you into a place where you recognize the power that you already have in the life that our loving Father has designed for you. God loves you, He has had a plan for you since the beginning and He is willing to reveal His plans for you to embrace. He wants you to enjoy His abundant life. He wants you to mature into the fullness of Christ and be able to deal with life as an overcomer, not as a victim or failure. He wants you to serve Him with joy in your heart. He wants you to live a satisfying life that impacts many around you maximally. He wants you to be His image and to reflect His glory and He wants the body of Christ to be a reflection of His glory.

Empowerment

Depending on your background, the word *empower* might have been used in various ways to describe a transfer of power. As a matter of fact you might have been empowered by a government body, an organization, or a group of people in the past, and you might have had a clear understanding of what actually happened when you were named the head of a department. You were given the authority to make decisions and act on behalf of that department within the jurisdiction of your responsibilities.

While your experience of empowerment or lack of it might be accurate, it might set this into perspective for you. It might help to get you to see the empowerment that has been made available to you as a child of the Most High. While there are different levels of fulfillments in having some kind of power, it cannot replace the satisfaction that you gain (daily) from knowing and entering into the empowerment that God graciously bestows on you.

Now the question is: what is Empowerment and what is it not? Who is it for? How can we access this empowerment? How do you know you have been empowered? We tackle these and many more questions like these in this book.

The Merriam-Webster Dictionary defines **empower** as to give power to (someone) or to give official authority or legal power to (someone). In the context of our topic, Empower is a supernatural action by God . As we proceed, you will see in the light of the scriptures that in Christ you already have access to God's grace and empowerment.

Grace

You may have been saying grace ever since you were a child, or you may know every scripture verse in which *grace* is mentioned, but these cannot substitute actually knowing in a revelatory way, what the *grace* of God is capable of in the life of a renewed child of God. If you know the definition of *grace* as unmerited favor, you are correct, but is that where it ends? Certainly not! God's grace did not just show up at Calvary, it has been in existence since way back in the famous Garden of Eden.

Again the Merriam-Webster Dictionary defines *grace* in the following way:
1. Unmerited divine assistance given human for their regeneration and sanctification.

2. Approval, special favor, pardon, mercy, privilege and a temporary exemption.

If you have not yet understood that by faith you have been pardoned for any wrong you have done or will do because of God's grace, then keep reading because you will soon discover that the silent script in your head no longer has the rights to torment you. Why? Because of what Jesus did.

The grace of God is the character of God, and the power of God. It is like having God himself. It is the strength of God and is available to you and I.

You may say, "I believe all that. You surely don't think you are telling me anything new!" I don't hope to tell you very much that is new; I only hope to set the table for you, arranging the dishes a little better and a little more attractively so that you will be tempted to partake of the feast. [2]

God has empowered you in Christ. You will see what part you have to play in this process and what God's part is. Being a great Christian is living a life that is empowered by the grace of God through Christ. The kind of life that impacts others to embrace the same kind of life of peace and rest in God Himself.

We have way too many people that are playing it safe while pretending to be waiting on God. There are Christians that are experiencing God's empowerment in certain areas of their lives but not in other areas. However, what God has in mind for us is to live as He would in every area of our lives. How many Christians do you know that are either fearful or doubtful about the abilities they have in Christ? It's alarming to see the defeat that is apparent in the lives of those that have been declared as Overcomers. Victors living as victims to things they have been given charge over.

As you go through the pages of this book, you will

find many helpful ideas and practical steps to help you to achieve them. We pray that God through His Holy Spirit will open your eyes to see every area in which you are living short of God's true riches for you, and that as your revelation comes, you will receive power to walk in His steps along your way of life.

Lord, we pray that through the study of Your word and the guidance of this writing, the percentage of believers that operate, as victors will increase and the impact that You want for our world will greatly increase. So that many more can be attracted to the glory that is in walking with You.

---

[2] Quote from "Tozer on Christian Leadership". A 366-Day Devotional. Compiled by Ronald Eggert. © 2001 by Christian Publications, Inc. ISBN: 0-87509-902-5

1. The Original Plan

Each time I read the account of the Creation, I cannot cease to be amazed at the intentionality with which God made all things. First, that God could see possibilities in the midst of the chaos. Everything was without form and void. But instead of stopping at the mess, God was looking through to see what he could create out of the mess.

Second, that God had an excellent ability to see things that were not yet in existence as though they were, so when He decided to create the things He saw, they could only be good. Notice how after each day of creation God looked at what He had made and it was good.

The Grace of God was in action throughout creation. I see an outstandingly creative God that could come up with such solutions from nothing. I often wonder how God's mind works. Of course, because I was made in His own image and I know my actions usually start from my mind, I figure His must too. Whenever I have a new idea, my heart beats faster with excitement; I can't wait to see my idea as a real thing. I can imagine this was in the 'behind the scenes' version of Genesis chapter one.

He was creating a new world, a huge world! Not only the features, characteristics, size, props of the universe, but also its contents. He was also creating the experiences inhabitants of the earth would have. Not just the experience of a person's lifetime but that of many generations. Science is still discovering many of the things created in Genesis chapter one. God arranged everything and put them in their position.

In the scene preceding the creation of man, notice how He called the attention of His members, giving them His line of thought. Isn't that what we call team spirit and great leadership? I noticed that the accounts of the other creation did not involve that or at least it was not recorded that He called His members. The record show instead that after He created this and He created that, He saw it was good.

However, the story changed when He was about to create you. He called all the members of His team together. This could be because of the fact that He wanted each member's image and nature to be reflected in this new masterpiece – you; He wanted each member of the trinity to be involved with Him in this special creation. He wanted you to have the image of the Father, Son and the Holy Spirit. And it could be that this next creation was so important and crucial to the continuity of the world; that this new creation was the one to represent Him among all the other creation - to dominate and subdue the earth.

There was definitely an excitement in God's plan of creating man. It was like He created man to enjoy all that He had created. God was doing this not so that

He could leave man to run the world by himself. Rather, the plan was supposed to rest on the fact that God was going to be in the midst of it all. Man was going to need God to complete His own tasks. The connection with God would determine the progress of man in his new world. There was a missing piece in man, a void that only God could fill.

We will address this further in a later chapter. The human being was made with the freedom to recognize what's important to him/her; made to choose God daily and not forced to love Him.

Now, notice how God, after creating man (male and female), blessed them:

"Prosper! Reproduce! Fill the Earth! Take charge! Be responsible for fish in the sea and birds in the air, for every living thing that moves on the face of the earth."
Genesis 1: 28 MSG

Wow! Note the way God empowered you even from the beginning. Isn't it interesting to note that this empowerment was so important that it came immediately after creation? You may say that was Adam and Eve, not me. Well, my prayer is that by the time you are done reading this book you would have started writing down your next line of action in line with God's blessings in Genesis one and thereafter.

God then showed them all the provision He had made for them, what would enable them to fulfill the blessings He had just pronounced upon them. What an empowered species we are! Of course in this section I also note that God said the plant was for our food, not animals. That's another interesting topic right there but not for this book. There are some good studies done already on this topic. I will add some to a blog post on another day. But for now, I want you to appreciate how much planning brought about the existence of human race. It didn't just start with your Mom and Dad.

Now, not putting Adam and Eve (our many generations back great grandparents) on the spot here, but I thought they were really empowered for greatness but for some reason they could not live up to the challenge. They did not see things clearly. This is the same reason why many live less than they were designed to be even today.

Adam and Eve clearly did not see the excellent plan that God had for them. They saw everything that was made available but they were daunted by the details in their lives.

"Prosper! Reproduce! Fill the Earth! Take charge! Be Responsible..."

Let me ask you a question: If a renowned man/woman of God (someone that you really respect) is having a meeting in your city and personally called you up for prayers. How do you respond to such prayers? Do you start running knowing that God's blessings have rested upon you and nothing can stop you now? Adam and Even had God (the Almighty) bless them and what did they do?

Empowered by Grace: The Void

2. Image and Likeness

If you agree with me (actually with the Bible) that man (human being) was made in the image and likeness of God, then you will also agree with me that man is capable of doing amazing things just like God. This explains why we see so many great things happening in our world. Many great ideas and inventions come out daily. Each generation since the beginning until now has experienced the emergence of people who chose to stand out in the crowd.

They recognize in whose image they were made and so they step into His shoes. In different variation people shine in their own ways. Big and small; they thrive locally and globally.

Before going further, let us dig into Genesis 1 to see what being created in God's image really means, let us identify some of the characteristics of God with which you were created. The list below is not exhaustive, but it gives an idea of what being created in the image of God means.

The following are my own interpretation of God's character in Genesis chapter one:

1. **Clearly identified the state of things-** *the earth was without form and void and darkness was over the face of the deep (Gen. 1:2)*
2. **Studied the current state** - *the Spirit of God was hovering over the face of the waters (Gen. 1:2).*
3. **Saw beyond the mess** – *the Spirit of God was hovering over the face of the waters (Gen. 1:2).*
4. **Came up with solutions to the problems** – *And God said, "Let there be light," and there was light (Gen. 1:3).*

5. **His words were powerful and creative –** *And God said, "Let there be light," and there was light (Gen. 1:3).*
6. **Thought clearly even in the midst of a major creation.** – *And God saw that the light was good. And God separated the light from the darkness (Gen. 1:4).*
7. **Happy with Himself and confident about His work** – *and*
8. **Analyzed His work even as He proceeded** – *And God saw that the light was good. And God separated the light from the darkness. God called the light Day, and the darkness he called Night. And there was evening and there was morning, the first day (Gen 1:4- 5).*
9. **He created to enrich others** - *And God said, "Let the waters swarm with swarms of living creatures, and let birds fly above the earth across the expanse of the heavens." So God created the great sea creatures and every living creature that moves, with which the waters swarm, according to their kinds, and*

every winged bird according to its kind. And God saw that it was good. And God blessed them, saying, "Be fruitful and multiply and fill the waters in the seas, and let birds multiply on the earth (Gen. 1:20-22)

10. **Clearly spoke His intentions and ideas** *Then God said, "Let us make man in our image, after our likeness. And let them have dominion over the fish of the sea and over the birds of the heavens and over the livestock and over all the earth and over every creeping thing that creeps on the earth (Gen. 1:26).*

11. **Carried His team members along** *Then God said, "Let us make man in our image, after our likeness (Gen. 1:26a).*

12. **Empowered human beings** - *And God blessed them. And God said to them, "Be fruitful and multiply and fill the earth and subdue it, and have dominion over the fish of the sea and over the birds of the heavens and over every living thing that moves on the earth (Gen. 1:28).*

13. **Blessed human beings** - *And God blessed them. And God said to them, "Be fruitful and multiply and fill the earth and subdue it, and have dominion over the fish of the sea and over the birds of the heavens and over every living thing that moves on the earth." And God said, "Behold, I have given you every plant yielding seed that is on the face of all the earth, and every tree with seed in its fruit. You shall have them for food (Gen. 1:28-29).*

As I earlier stated, the list above is not exhaustive. As a matter of fact, when we talk about God, He is new every morning. When someone else reads the same chapter of the Bible they can get many other characteristics of God that I didn't mention here. The same will happen at another time for me, this is God and His word - new every morning.

Look around you, among people you know, do you see people that are making a mark, doing awesome things like God? They have recognized what they are capable of and are doing it.

I read the story of a little 9-year-old boy, whose dad had a used auto parts store. He went to the shop with his dad during his summer vacation. One day he got an idea to create his own cardboard arcade machine. He got all the carton boxes and other supplies that he would need: scissors, nets, strings, tapes, glue, markers, all of them. One day at a time he worked so that over time he had created his very own arcade-the first ever-grand cardboard arcade. And he also created the token to play on his arcade and the tickets for the rewards. He made a price list: with $1 you can play 4 rounds and with $2 you get his fun pass which allows you to play 500 rounds that expires in one month.

For many days, he played his arcade alone because not many clients were walking into his father's shop anyway. One day, a man walked in looking for an auto part for his old car and saw the arcade machine on the side. He asked the boy about it and after explaining to him the man bought a $2 deal. He was so fascinated that he came back with a camera crew and got a video of this boy which he posted on YouTube and some other sites. The story of this boy went viral on the Internet. People lined up for hours waiting to play this little boy's cardboard arcade and he raised over $130,000 (for the boy's education) through sales and online donations.

There are many more stories like this on Motivationalvideos.me. Great people are creating new things daily. Some of these people are in remote villages where no one can find them while others are privileged to be all over the Internet. My focus is not on fame but on impact and influence.

One thing these people have in common is that they recognize that they have a treasure inside of them that can impact the world around them so they go for it. It usually starts by either solving a problem they personally have or helping someone around them. While they are at it, they find that a few other people need what they are offering so they make more and get either more impact or more money in return.

They believe in themselves and they engage themselves in order to achieve the ideas on their minds. They sow and they reap. They invest all their resources. By following natural rules and principles, they get results. They sow their thoughts, their time, their money, their originality and they reap great results.

These people believe that great things can come out of them the way they are. They are not trying to be like others. They assess themselves correctly. If all they think they have is a mind that can create funny stuffs, they don't ignore it to pursue something else. Instead, they create with what comes naturally to them. This makes it easy for them to be comfortable as they create.

You must realize that many of these people did not plan to be great, they just liked the package that they got (their uniqueness) and they thrive on discovering more about themselves.

However, at this point let me re-emphasize that the original plan was not that man would thrive on his own. There was an even greater plan. He needed God. And God was willing to share His life with man. God simply didn't want to force man into a compulsory relationship with Him. He wanted man to make that personal decision to connect with Him daily.

Empowered by Grace: The Void

3. The Void & the Pseudo Power

Have you ever being in touch with a visionary? Someone that has a vision and goes on to start a mission? Whether it's a business or a non-profit, there is something evident about them. They have a clear understanding of how their mission is supposed to run. They know the details. As a matter of fact, they are the only one that can pass along the correct information to anyone that ever wants to help in the mission. Imagine what happens when the visionary passes on. A void is created and the work may suffer.

The surviving team members try to make things work using all the information available to them. Despite their struggle and hard work, very few missions are sustained after the visionary departs. If they survive they do so in another form. The people left behind enter the scene doing what they are good at and focus usually on some other features of the mission, disposing of the previous idea.

Whenever a creator makes something, he has a big role to play in the functionality of that thing. In the original plan, God's plan was not exclusive to God. He was intended to be a major part of the universe. He was meant to be a vital part of man's life. He had a big picture of what He was trying to achieve with the universe. This is why when you look at Genesis 1, and you read "God said it was good" after each creation, you should ask: " good in relation to what?" It was in relation to the big picture God had in mind.

Take God out and nothing is complete anymore, very similar to taking the visionary out and creating a void in the mission. Man was made to thrive in perfect relation with God. This is like a puzzle with a perfect centerpiece. Take away the centerpiece and the puzzle is incomplete. With God being the center of the whole plan, nothing was created to exist without God.

In other words, man was created in relation to God. Therefore because of this, man was designed to reflect the image of God as he relates to Him. This is why apparent in every man is a void that God must fill. The relationship with God was vital for your success. This is also similar to what you see in any powered toy. There is a space in the toy to add power so it can do all that it was designed to. If you add the required batteries, it functions perfectly but if you take out the batteries you take out the life of the toy.

This reminds me of a toy spaceship that we got for our son when he was very little. This toy would teach him about animals, colors, shapes, and numbers. When powered appropriately, it does some amazing stuff. When you turn it on, it starts with something like "Welcome I am the learning spaceship, what do you want to learn today?" When you select animals for example, it says "Animal, animal" then it says select the lion, if you identify the lion correctly it says "That is a lion, yay!!" Then it goes "select the monkey!" if you don't get it right it would say "that is a lion, select the elephant"... It was cute. It also had sounds that entertained the kids. However, it could be annoying to adults after a while and if you left it on and inactive, it would occasionally wake itself up and say "See you next time, bye-bye". It was programmed to do that in order to go into the sleep mode.

Many times we would forget to turn it off and so in the middle of the night we would wake up to a high pitched-voice saying "See you next time, bye-bye". How annoying! One night I got up, found the screwdriver and took out the batteries. I had had enough. Of course by the time my son got to his toy thereafter, he was disappointed that he couldn't hear the toy speak any more. He fiddled with it for a while, tossed it around wondering what was wrong.

For that period he would play with this spaceship but not so much as a learning toy but the type that you bang and toss around.

This happened for many weeks and the excitement he had for the toy wore off until one day, many weeks later when I put the batteries back in again. The boy, who by now had forgotten what his toy was capable of, was so shocked to rediscover its full use.

When I took out the batteries I created a void in this toy that could only be filled with the required batteries. Just like this spaceship, you were made with a void and this was part of the design. God Himself wanted to fill this void. Though God made man to be powerful and able to stand by himself, he would be his best only when the perfect piece of the puzzle (God) is in place, when he is fully connected to God in great fellowship. When God is the source of man's life, the one on the throne of man's heart.

Ralph Neighbour explains it clearly in his book, *Beginning the Journey* that:

> When you become a Christian, you gave your life to Jesus Christ to become not only your savior, but also your Lord. That means you have given up all rights to your life. You continually confess, "Jesus is Lord!" [3]

Using my toy illustration, the manner in which the toy was unable to function at its best, is that same way a human being without God is not at its best. There is even misuse or abuse when the proper centerpiece of the puzzle is missing.

Satan recognized this void was there and that Man was designed with the free will to decide what he chooses to fill his void with. So he preyed on this, Satan approached Eve with an amazing offer:

Now the serpent was more crafty than any other beast of the field that the Lord God had made.

He said to the woman, "Did God actually say, 'You shall not eat of any tree in the garden'?"

He sowed a doubt in her heart.

And the woman said to the serpent, "We may eat of the fruit of the trees in the garden, but God said, 'You shall not eat of the fruit of the tree that is in the midst of the garden, neither shall you touch it, lest you die.'" But the serpent said to the woman, "You will not surely die. For God knows that when you eat of it your eyes will be opened, and you will be like God, knowing good and evil."

He encouraged her to misuse her free will and promised her something that seemed better than God's plan.

So when the woman saw that the tree was good for food, and that it was a delight to the eyes, and that the tree was to be desired to make one wise, she took of its fruit and ate, and she also gave some to her husband who was with her, and he ate. Then the eyes of both were opened, and they knew that they were naked. And they sewed fig leaves together and made themselves loincloths (Genesis 3:1-7)

Satan made an offer for Eve, What I have for you will give you authority, recognition and value in life- You will no longer need God but you will become like God. Eve must have rationalized it like most of us women. *"This might actually save me some stress of spending time to be with God, it might actually help me when I need something on the spot, I won't need to have to meet with God, and you mean I will know everything? Wow! I want that!"* She must have thought it was going to be an addition. "*I mean, I won't lose anything right? I will just add more wealth to myself*". Not knowing that it was not an addition but a substitution, she said yes to the devil's offer and lost the connection they had with God.

Interestingly, though man was made to be like God, when sin came into the picture, man removed God from the throne of His life. He chose to be in charge of his life or that was what he thought. The truth though, is that since he listened to the devil, he was now under the devil's rule to a large extent. He had lost his position, and rights with God and was now subject to the enemy's torture or counsel.

It is very interesting to know that the same temptation that Satan used to get Eve and Adam did not end there. When the Lord Jesus was about to start his Ministry on earth, the devil being very crafty, also had an amazing offer for him in Matthew 4:1-7 below:

Then Jesus was led up by the Spirit into the wilderness to be tempted by the devil. And after fasting forty days and forty nights, he was hungry. And the tempter came and said to him, "If you are the Son of God, command these stones to become loaves of bread."

First, the devil tried to sow a doubt in Jesus about his position in God and then tried to convince him to meet his own physical needs first before anything else.

But he answered, "It is written,

"'Man shall not live by bread alone, but by every word that comes from the mouth of God.

Then the devil took him to the holy city and set him on the pinnacle of the temple and said to him, "If you are the Son of God, throw yourself down, for it is written, "'He will command his angels concerning you,' and "'On their hands they will bear you up, lest you strike your foot against a stone.'"

Then the devil tried to convince Jesus to misuse his rights, his free will, his authority.

Jesus said to him, "Again it is written, 'You shall not put the Lord your God to the test.'" Again, the devil took him to a very high mountain and showed him all the kingdoms of the world and their glory. And he said to him, "All these I will give you, if you will fall down and worship me."

Then the devil claimed to have everything in the world and was willing to give them to Jesus if only he would remove God from the place of authority in his life.

Then Jesus said to him, "Be gone, Satan! For it is written, "'You shall worship the Lord your God and him only shall you serve.'" Then the devil left him, and behold, angels came and were ministering to him.

Isn't it very interesting that the devil was offering Jesus the same thing he offered Eve in Genesis? Well, the truth of the matter is that, if you study history, you will find that that same strategy has been used with everyone, including yourself. The devil recognizes the void in man and always offers that he has a better option for filling the void in man's life. He always promises to give a power that He does not even possess. He promises to empower man to be his best.

Depending on where you are today, where you have been, what you have done, and what has been done to you, you will most likely remember a point where you were faced with similar temptations. You might even be struggling with a similar situation now and you are wondering what to do. The point is that you have a void and you will always need to fill that void.

There are so many things competing for your attention so you can fill your void with them. If you get those red shoes, you will be so powerful. If you take this course, you will become financially strong. If you take this medicine, you will be strong physically. If you purchase this get-away package, your marriage will become one of the best. All these things promise to empower you. But is this really the missing puzzle piece?

Take a moment to recollect some of the episodes you have had in your past: a time when you felt you were going to become more fulfilled, happier, richer... and then you got what you were looking for. Did you actually feel satisfied after that? Only for a moment. I am almost sure you wanted something more immediately afterward. More money, more time, more love, more friends, more skills, more knowledge, more achievements, the list goes on. If you have not reconnected back to God and allowed Him to be the One on the throne of your life, you will always have that desire for more.

When sin came in, there appeared a gap between God and man; a gap that left a void in man. This void is the cause of many failures and problems in our world today. Personally, when I retrace all my errors and I see that this void is the reason for them all.

The void is represented or displayed in various

human needs. They form the root cause of every problem, every error, and every problem on earth. If you know the root of each thought or action you will be in a better position to properly deal with them. You would be able to identify unique needs and satisfy them accordingly. Every man/ woman/ child has the following needs that they are trying to meet daily.

Everyone wants to be:

- Accepted
- Acknowledged
- Admired
- Appreciated
- Approved of
- Challenged
- Empowered
- Free
- Happy
- Heard
- Important
- In control
- Independent
- Knowledgeable
- Listened to
- Loved
- Needed

- Noticed
- Powerful
- Productive
- Proud
- Reassured
- Recognized
- Relaxed
- Respected
- Safe
- Satisfied
- Secure
- Significant
- Supported
- Treated fairly
- Understood
- Useful
- Valued
- Worthy

Each person sets out to meet these needs daily. When all is said and done if God is not the One that meets this needs in your life, you will find that life can become a rat race. You experience frustration upon frustration. For example, an individual who feel significance because he just got a good job and tries to meet this need through his job, may get frustrated by his boss or colleague, gets married to feel stronger may also enters another level of stress. The stress continues even when they go on that well-deserved vacation to Bahamas? Nothing is able to permanently quench our thirst for the human needs above. God alone is the perfect piece that can quench all thirst.

---

[3] Quote from "Beginning the Journey, Entering the kingdom of God" by Ralph W. Neighbour Jr. and Jim Egli. Revised Edition 2001. Published by touch Publications.

4. Grace at Calvary and Beyond

And they heard the sound of the Lord God walking in the garden in the cool of the day, and the man and his wife hid themselves from the presence of the Lord God among the trees of the garden. But the Lord God called to the man and said to him, "Where are you?"
Genesis 3:8-9 ESV

Man was created to need God and at the same time man had a place in God's heart. It was a two-way relationship. God enjoyed coming around to have fun in the garden with His people and they knew He was coming and were excited each time. God was longing for their time together, and they were looking forward to it. I can imagine that as soon as they heard Him coming on a normal day, even if they planned to do a little hide and seek game with Him, they were excited to see Him. They had a void

- God and only God could fill it. Just like that of a person looking forward to seeing their lover again, they looked forward to being with God each time.

However, the day talked about in the passage above was different. God had to call out for them. Why? He must have noticed that the place they filled in Him was empty. Like the terminal guard that cannot get the signals from a certain aircraft and calls out to see if they can hear him, God said "Where are you?" In this case, they could hear Him but they knew they had lost a connection and He felt the same.

For all have sinned and fall short of the glory of God
Romans 3:23 ESV

Man lost the connection and he also lost his position with God. To God man became dead. He could no long hear God or fellowship with Him. Just like that plane that lost connection is no longer in the terminal's radar; man died to God.

You may say, well I was not the one that sinned so this death should not apply to me. Wrong! When we say man lost connection we mean human being lost their place or connection that was available before. And so the human kind (the specie human) could no longer connect with God, forming the void in every child, man & woman.

And you were dead in the trespasses and sins in which you once walked, following the course of this world, following the prince of the power of the air, the spirit that is now at work in the sons of disobedience— among whom we all once lived in the passions of our flesh, carrying out the desires of the body and the mind, and were by nature children of wrath, like the rest of mankind. But God, being rich in mercy, because of the great love with which he loved us, even when we were dead in our trespasses, made us alive together with Christ— by grace you have been saved
Ephesians 2: 1-5 ESV

God being so rich in mercy, love, and grace created a new way out for man to be reunited with him. The former plan could no longer be used because man was dead to God and now had a limited life span. God had to create a new way and so Jesus came and died in our place and in dying He paid the ransom that Satan required and set us free from the debt we owed the slave master.

> *...and raised us up with him and seated us with him in the heavenly places in Christ Jesus.*
> *Ephesians 2: 6 ESV*

We regained our connection back to God but this time through His one and only son-Jesus.

> *Therefore, since we have been justified by faith, we have peace with God through our Lord Jesus Christ. Through him we have also obtained access by faith into this grace in which we stand, and we rejoice in hope of the glory of God.*

Romans 5:1-2. ESV

God is so full of mercy. He created us in His image and had a plan but His plan was thwarted because He did not want to command love from us, which made Him to give us a free will to choose Him. Then again in His great grace and mercy, He created a way to promote us back to the place He had for us but this time through his son.

I just heard a story today (as I write) about a village in Nigeria where some 14-25 people suddenly died. The World Health Organization's correspondence said they were sure it was not Ebola (a deadly virus that affected some part of Africa recently). The report states that the victims did not show any symptoms of vomiting and diarrhea, which are signs of Ebola. These people mysteriously all lost their sight and died shortly afterwards.

Some closer news reported that these people had gone to a local shrine to steal some materials and so the god of the land dealt with them mercilessly. As much as I am not sure what is true about this story, I am led to see the horror from the gods of this world. No mercy for sin, no grace against judgments. Sin and die. Thanks to God for making a way out to be free again for everyone that believes.

"For God so loved the world, that he gave his only Son, that whoever believes in him should not perish but have eternal life.
John 3:16 ESV

So that, through faith, (the kind that comes from understanding what Christ did), every man can have the amazing life of Christ. Free from the requirements of sin from the devil. Free from every guilt of sin and free to be like Christ.

> *And you will know the truth, and the truth will set you free.*
> *John 8:32 ESV*

What an amazing place to be!

All sin, all record of sin, all shame, all guilt was paid for. Every man that accepts what Christ did is free to live in Christ.

> *Therefore, if anyone is in Christ, he is a new creation. The old has passed away; behold, the new has come.*
> *2 Corinthians 5:17 ESV*

That is why the life after Calvary is an amazing life, an abundant life. If you are yet to be reconnected to God through Christ, you are missing out on life. When you let Christ sit fully on the throne of your life, life will then become fulfilling. Note that I said you let Christ sit fully on the throne of your life. This is what we call being born again, being a

Christian, or regenerated. Unfortunately, not everyone that claims to be born again is actually enjoying the freedom and empowerment that is in Christ.

Many that know Christ and billions that do not are equally suffering. Some succeed because they have recognized that they are capable of succeeding, but then they need more. They succeed but they always need more achievements to get more fulfillment. They do all that lies within their power to get what they want. They enter the rat race and they try to become the best in the race.

Some Christians on the other hand, that have refused to hand their throne over to Christ fall into the same trap. They keep trying but because they are not being empowered by Christ, they come short of the glory that is already theirs. Doubt, fear, pain, shame, guilt, forgiveness, bitterness, lack of patience, lack of zeal, wrong self-judgment, wrong judgment of others, lack of faith, anger, laziness, pride and many things like these stand in the way of many Christians. Some are even crippled by what they call faith, but what I call misplaced faith.

Some Christians, in the name of believing God for the perfect instruction, or should I say waiting for God to speak to them like he did with Samuel (I Samuel 3) or Balaam's donkey (Numbers 22: 17-41) would not step out in faith. All the while they say they are waiting for a perfect instruction before they can ever do anything. You have God as your boss, what could go wrong if the One that created all things is inside of you. The only important thing would be to keep a clear view of Him.

Life beyond the cross is an empowered life. You are no longer alive but Christ now lives in you.

I have been crucified with Christ. It is no longer I who live, but Christ who lives in me. And the life I now live in the flesh I live by faith in the Son of God, who loved me and gave himself for me.

Galatians 2:20 ESV

Guess what? You are in great company. Seated in the heavenly places...

That the God of our Lord Jesus Christ, the Father of glory, may give you the Spirit of wisdom and of revelation in the knowledge of him, having the eyes of your hearts enlightened, that you may know what is the hope to which he has called you, what are the riches of his glorious inheritance in the saints, and what is the immeasurable greatness of his power toward us who believe, according to the working of his great might that he worked in Christ when he raised him from the dead and seated him at his right hand in the heavenly places, far above all rule and authority and power and dominion, and above every name that is named, not only in this age but also in the one to come. And he put all things under his feet and gave him as head over all things to the church.
Ephesians 1:17-22 ESV

5. Your New Identity

Therefore, if anyone is in Christ, he is a new creation; old things have passed away; behold, all things have become new.
2 Corinthians. 5:17 NKJ

During my (Ade) Masters of Engineering program at Concordia University in Canada, I needed to go with some other students to the United States for an IEEE conference. I applied for the visa and, to my surprise, it was denied. I was really disappointed and I decided that I would not apply for a US visa anymore because my applications were already in to become a permanent resident of Canada. I knew that as a permanent resident of Canada I could visit the USA without a visa. To cut the long story short, I became a permanent resident and still could not visit the USA without a visa because the US changed their policy in the wake of the 9-11 terrorist attacks so I had to wait until I became a Canadian citizen. I can still remember the first time I drove to the USA with my Canadian Citizenship card and my driver's license. It felt really good to see the Immigration officer give my card back and say have a nice trip.

Why am I sharing this story? It is because God has used it to remind me of my citizenship of God's Kingdom from time to time. I did not feel any change in my life over those years that I waited to become a citizen of Canada. There is no special feeling that accompanies a change in status, or citizenship. It simply is a fact that is recognized by the authorities around you. Your status as a believer does not come with a special feeling. It is a fact recognized by the spiritual authorities around you.

Do you remember when you turned 18 years of age? One week before that you are not permitted to vote and the next week you are and not only that, there are lots of responsibilities and privileges that become applicable to you.

In this chapter I would like to draw your attention to the fact that as a believer in the Lord Jesus, there are so many blessings that you have access to. Your new life in Christ Jesus gives you access to everything that is in Christ Jesus. You can tap into the wisdom of God, the resources of heaven, help from fellow believers, love, peace and joy in abundance and much greater impact than your mind can conceive. You may not feel that this is true, you may not even understand how it is possible but those are not relevant to your ability to access these blessings and live a much more joyful and impactful life.

So what do we do now?

1) Agree that you are in Christ Jesus and as a result all that belongs to Christ and His followers belong to you!

This is by far the most important step. If you do not believe, you will not act. If you act just to that you say you did, you will face oppositions and you will stop. You must really read over the previous chapters as well as the verses presented below and agree that they are talking about you and no one else.

"As the Father loved Me, I also have loved you; abide in My love.
John 15:9 NKJ

Thoughts - Jesus loves me! I am precious to GOD!

Who shall separate us from the love of Christ? Shall tribulation... For I am persuaded that neither death nor life, nor angels nor principalities nor powers, nor things present nor things to come, nor height nor depth, nor any other created thing, shall be able to separate us from the love of God which is in Christ Jesus our Lord.
Romans 8:35-39 NKJ

Thought - Nothing can separate me from the love of Christ!

Blessed be the God and Father of our Lord Jesus Christ, who has blessed us with every spiritual blessing in the heavenly places in Christ, just as He chose us in Him before the foundation of the world, that we should be holy and without blame before Him in love,
Ephesians 1:3-4 NKJ

Thought - I am blessed! There is no blessing I need that is not available to me. I am chosen by God to be holy and without blame before Him in love. God makes me holy and blameless in Christ.

In Him we have redemption through His blood, the forgiveness of sins, according to the riches of His grace
Ephesians 1:7 NKJ

Thought - I am forgiven!

> *He has delivered us from the power of darkness and conveyed us into the kingdom of the Son of His love, in whom we have redemption through His blood, the forgiveness of sins.*
> *Col 1:13-14 NKJ*

Thought - I have been delivered from the power of darkness! I have been brought into God's Kingdom! My sins are all forgiven through the blood of Jesus.

I once wrote a cheque for a brother – I would call him John here - I wrote the cheque to the bank and at the back of the cheque I asked that the money be transferred into his account. This was because he did not have a checking account through which he could process the cheque. As soon as he saw the unusual way that the cheque was written, he let me know that the cheque would not be honored. I assured him that it would. I was surprised to see the man come in after about 40 minutes with the cheque claiming that it was not honored. Why would it not be honored I asked? "Well the cashier said they can't do it" he replied. So I called the bank, told them what had happened, they apologized and asked the man to return. Needless to say, the cheque was honored and he got his money. I believe this situation happened so that I, as well as you, can learn that when we do not believe the truth, it may not work for us not because it does not work, but because we do not believe enough to apply ourselves.

Why did John get his money the second time? Because he was sure that the cheque could be honored. While he doubted, every little resistance was enough to discourage him. When you believe the word of God as revealed in scriptures, it gives you strength to insist on enjoying your blessing.

Let me state it again - As a believer you are entitled to everything that is in Christ - love, joy, peace, fruitfulness, impact, wisdom, grace, the miraculous, and much more. You can find all these in scriptures and books that have been written on this topic.

It is important to note however that we also partake of the persecution and prejudice that Jesus receives. If we are in Christ Jesus, we get what He gets.

2) Practice what you believe.

I hope you agree now that whatever the Scriptures declare that we have in Christ Jesus is actually available to you. If you believe then you will need to start acting in line with your belief. It's true that there may be lots of doubtful thoughts that will go through your mind, however I would like to encourage you to follow what the word says consistently until you start to experience what you believe.

Do you believe that God is your Heavenly Father? Then practice that truth. Talk to God like you would talk to a Heavenly Father! Do you believe that God loves you? Then connect with God with an understanding that He loves you. Respond to the love of God by expressing gratitude, love, and commitment. Do you believe that God is almighty, all-powerful? Then respond to Him like that. Act in line with the truth that there is nothing impossible for God to do.

Practicing what you believe can be scary at first because you will have to act against what your natural senses tell you. You will have to act like a winner when everything around you tells you that you are failing and you will fail. When I say act like a winner, I do not mean pretend to be a winner! I mean, see yourself winning and do the hard work and smart work that is necessary for someone who knows that with God all things are possible.

Many times we get defeated not because we did not have what it took to win, but because there were too many voices and forces that reminded us that we were failures and, for some reason or the other, we chose to side with those voices and we gave up. It's time to start increasing the number of voices that remind you that you are no longer a failure, you are no longer average, you are not even very good, you are excellent because God has made His excellence available to you.

To do this, you will need to read the verses listed above every day. You should place them on your mirror or somewhere on your phone where you can see them every day. Meditate on those scriptures and visualize the implications of those truths in your life. Rejoice over the fact that it is done already through Jesus Christ and give thanks to God for them. As you do this daily, you will find your faith increasing and the voice of the Holy Spirit will become louder and stronger in your ears reminding you that in Christ Jesus, you are more than a conqueror.

I do not want you to assume that just reading through this book will make a big difference in your life. It will initiate the change, but it is the consistent practice of the truth you believe that makes the difference. Determine to start living in the reality of your new identity today.

3) Be patient to receive the reward

And we desire that each one of you show the same diligence to the full assurance of hope until the end, that you do not become sluggish, but imitate those who through faith and patience inherit the promises.
(Hebrews 6:11-12 NKJ)

As you begin to act in line with your new identity, you may discover that things do not start to change around you immediately. You may still find that your joy is not full from time to time, that people have not become nicer and that some of the mistakes you have made previously have not disappeared.

Do not be alarmed or discouraged by what you see or experience at this point. It took so many years to get to where you are now. You have developed many habits and attitudes that helped you to survive as a non-believer in the Lord Jesus Christ. It may take some time for you to completely break off these habits and also for the effects of all those years of ignorance to wear off. So be patient and continue to act according to what the scriptures says about you and in due time - not very long at all- you will see the fruit of your new identity.

One immediate fruit that you will notice though is joy and peace. As long as you focus on what you have received in Christ Jesus, joy and peace will flood your heart. This joy and peace should be your proof that you believe the truth that is revealed in scriptures.

4) Remember you belong to God

Or do you not know that your body is the temple of the Holy Spirit who is in you, whom you have from God, and you are not your own? For you were bought

at a price; therefore glorify God in your body and in your spirit, which are God's.
(1 Corinthians 6:19-20 NKJ)

The truth that you are not your own may not sound very exciting at first because all of our lives we have been trying to prove that we are somebody! We desire to be seen as very significant and that in our absence we will be missed. You are not alone in this. However as the scriptures show us, we were created by God in His image! We actually belong to God! Yes, we got into doing things our own way, and we were lost but we have been redeemed! We still belong to God. True significance and impact can only be found in Christ. When you align yourself to God's plan for your life, you will find not only joy and peace but also significance and impact.

How does this affect your life now? For starters, your life ambitions and goals cannot be less than what God wants for you! If your life goals are what God wants for you, then you have a lot going for you because God is all-powerful. There is nothing impossible for Him. You also do not need to worry about current challenges, what you need to concern yourself with is that you are applying yourself consistently to the plan that God has designed for you.

As you continue to review the details from scriptures of all that you now have as a citizen of God's Kingdom, as a child in God's family, and one who belongs to God, you must come to terms with the truth that without Christ you can do nothing that will be of any eternal good. You must stop trying to make a name for yourself and rather begin to enjoy the truth that all the name you will ever need, you already have as a child of the almighty God and that all the significance and love you will ever need is already yours in Christ. Think of it, you are loved and accepted by God, He has done all that needs to be done to rescue you from your own rebellious life and from the lies of your enemy the devil. He delights to work with you and has a plan for your life. What more do you need?

You may say, but I need a spouse, a car, a home, a good job, something to live for! Yes, but all these are no more your primary responsibilities. They are all available in God and within His plan for your life. It pleases our Father to make all that we need available to us. As we delight in Him and surrender to His plans for us, all these things are added. They are no longer the source of our joy! We already have joy and peace from knowing that our future is secured in God. That no matter what happens all around us, we are already blessed because we are in Christ and He is in us.

The natural question that flows from the preceding discussion is then, how do I know what God's plan for my life is? How can I be sure that what I am doing is not just what I chose to do? The short answer is relationship! Yes, as you learn to respond to the love of God in your heart, you will also learn to discern the will of God for your life!

You will know when the joy of your heart begins to wane and when the confidence that you are doing God's will is being eroded. Of course you will not find the name of your spouse in the Bible, nor would you find the name of the company to work for or the model of car you should buy! You will need to make these decisions with an open heart. By this, I mean that you make your decisions while checking to know if that is what God wants for you. For example, if you find that you are gifted musically and you want to know whether to pursue a career in music or do some other things. You ask the Lord to guide you and at the same time you begin to prayerfully consider how a music career can be used to move the Kingdom of God forward and how your other options would also help. As you do this, you may see a clear path in one of the choices. If this is the case, then you choose that. In this case, let us say you settle for the other path (nursing). As soon as you decide on pursuing nursing, you think of the applications, you speak with the nurses or nursing students around you and read as much as you can about the career (all this time still being prayerful), if your joy continues to be full and you are actually looking forward to being accepted into the program, then you proceed with the choice.

You will also try to figure out how the musical talent can be used in tandem with the nursing career because God does not waste His gifts on us. He definitely has a plan to use every gift that He has given us. As you continue with your life, you must always check your heart to see that you are always ready to change plans or choose whatever God leads you to. This flexibility and readiness to adjust is what makes it easy to know what God's will is. It is God's delight to communicate His will to us.

6. Getting Out of the Rot

I love to study people and I have met quite a few in my short life. I try to find out why most people do what they do. I find that the psychology behind every action determines a lot about the action and its consequence.

I have met people that take life as it comes and others that give it their best. Some people hide under the umbrella of waiting on God for instructions and they drag their feet and get no results.

For so many years, I personally did not lay hold on God's grace for me and the result was an unfulfilled life. I dragged my feet to step out in faith. Though I served God with much dedication I was blinded by the need and urge to act right so much so that I did not allow the truth of the word of God penetrate deep into my heart in order for it to do a complete transformative work. Therefore, I failed many times to experience the thrills through the provision, which had always been in an abundant supply.

After many years of trying to meet my needs and filling my void with whatever else is exciting, I have discovered that by allowing God to meet my every need (as stated in the two previous chapters) is the only way out. As you allow Him to be all you need, He will point your heart to see His grace upon you then you will need to make up your mind to willingly follow His instructions every time. This is the very first step to living a life of great influence and impact that leads to fulfillments in life. God wants to pour into you daily. He wants you to:

"Prosper! Reproduce! Fill the Earth! Take charge! Be Responsible..."

He has given you the truth in His word (the Bible), He will guide you through His Holy Spirit to discover the truth and then He will enable you to activate and implement the truth in your daily life.

I will instruct you and teach you in the way you should go; I will counsel you with my eye upon you.
Psalms 32:8

Come, O children, listen to me; I will teach you the fear of the Lord.
Psalms 34:11

But the Helper, the Holy Spirit, whom the Father will send in my name, he will teach you all things and bring to your remembrance all that I have said to you.
John 14:26

Next, if you are ready to get out of the rot, you are willing to begin to step out and daringly become the man or woman that God made you; there are a few other things you need to get right. They are easy to achieve because Christ is ready to help you. Follow them like A, B, C, D…

1. **A**ccept Christ's offers for a life of influence.
2. **B**elieve that God has empowered you in Christ.
3. **C**ommit to clearly hearing from God everyday.
4. **D**etermine to do whatever you clearly understand as His instruction to you each time.
5. **E**xpress the original (unique and not fake) you to everyone you meet.
6. **F**ace each day as a victor and not a victim.
7. **G**ive the best from you everyday as if it were your last.
8. **H**ope for the best in others and help them.
9. **I**nitiate a desire for God (and dependence on Him) in the people you meet daily.
10. **J**ust live like Christ daily; enjoying your eternal life here on earth and on the other side of this life.

Again remember that if you have been in this rot for so long, it's going to take a lot to get out of it. Here are 2 main aspects that you have to allow God to deal with.

1. The way you think
2. What you do

The first, the way you think in general, will determine the way your life turns out.

Guard your heart above all else, for it determines the course of your life.
Proverbs 4:23 (NLT)

The way you think about God, about life, about yourself, about others. You must allow God to renew your mind with His word.

Do not be conformed to this world, but be transformed by the renewal of your mind, that by

testing you may discern what is the will of God, what is good and acceptable and perfect.
Romans 12:2

As a person of influence, you no longer think like everyone, you need to learn how to think with God's big picture in mind. As you allow God to change your perspectives you will see that you will begin to see others (including God, life, and yourself) differently. If you used to think that no one cares about you, God will help you to think otherwise.

First, that He really cares about you. Second, he will show you some other people that care about you as well, and how to gradually surround yourself with such people; those with same values as you. Read the previous chapter about your new identity over and over and meditate on the scriptures and others like them until faith arises in you dispelling every doubt.

The second aspect is changing what you do on a regular basis. God will shine His light to see the way you behave, allow Him. Usually your daily habits becomes your weekly habits and that becomes your monthly habits, and then yearly and then your lifetime habits. Check what you are doing today that you don't want to be seen as your identity and allow God to work on your daily habits in order to live an exceptional and influential life.

Here is a list I compiled on my launchadream.com website to show a difference between winners and losers:

Their Perspective

- Winners think about possibilities and ways to achieve. Losers focus on obstacles and on excuses that will stop them from achieving.
- Winners believe there is always a thing to learn. Losers consider themselves as an expert even though they know little.

- Winners find opportunities in crisis. Losers complain about crisis
- Winners enjoy being in the present and learn from the past. Losers live in the past
- Winners dream in the day. Losers dream in bed.
- Winners take responsibility. Losers blame others.
- Winners control their own destiny. Losers leave everything to their fate.
- Winners give more than they take. Losers take more than they give.
- Winners are not scared to walk alone if the crowd is walking in the wrong direction. Losers follow the crowd.

Their Habits

- Winners always plan. Losers hate having a plan.
- Winners set goals. Losers lack goals.
- Winners take action consistently. Losers refrain from taking action and lack consistency.

- Winners constantly expand their comfort zone. Losers remain in their comfort zone.
- Winners work hard. Losers avoid work.
- Winners try different strategies when not getting their expected results. Losers do the same thing over and over again expecting different results.
- Winners learn from their failures. Losers fear failure and avoid it at all cost.
- Winners listen. Losers fight for every chance to talk.
- Winners continue to develop their skill every other day without fail. Losers make little effort in developing their skill.
- Winners face their fear, accept it and take the leap. Losers dwell in their fear.
- Winners commit to only what they can give their best to. Losers make promises that they always break.

- Winners give their best at whatever thing they decide to do. Losers work half-heartedly in everything that they do.
- Winners are persistent and will do whatever it takes (ethically) to achieve their goal. Losers give up when obstacles pop up.
- Winners manage their time well and indulge in high value activities that will bring them closer to their goals. Losers indulge in time wasting activities like watching TV as long as they want.
- Winners always find a better way to do things. Losers stick to one way of doing things.
- Winners make personal development a priority. Losers neglect personal development.
- Winners spend money on seminars and classes to improve themselves. Losers think that spending money on seminars and classes is a waste of money and they prefer to buy things that give them instant gratification.

- Winners help others to win. Losers refuse to help and think only about their own benefit.
- Winners find like-minded people like themselves that can bring them to greater height. Losers find like-minded people like themselves that will drag them to failure.

In order to start living a fulfilled life today, you need to think like God and behave like God. Remember you were made in His image? Then start living like you really are His likeness.

> *Whatever you do, work heartily, as for the Lord and not for men.*
> *(Colossians 3:23 ESV)*

I am not claiming that hard work guarantees success. No! However, there is a great peace that comes into a life that is fully yielded to God's plan. You enter His rest. Not worrying anymore about living a life that is better than the Jones' but living a life that you were designed to live. You are no longer defeated by the stress and challenges that surround you. As long as you hear from the One that fits your void perfectly, you become strengthened by His grace alone.

Similar to what Paul recorded for us when He was begging God to take the thorn away from his flesh, you will see that His grace is all you need.

So to keep me from becoming conceited because of the surpassing greatness of the revelations, a thorn was given me in the flesh, a messenger of Satan to harass me, to keep me from becoming conceited. Three times I pleaded with the Lord about this, that it should leave me. But he said to me, "My grace is sufficient for you, for my power is made perfect in weakness." Therefore I will boast all the more gladly of my weaknesses, so that the power of Christ may rest upon me. For the sake of Christ, then, I am content with weaknesses, insults, hardships,

persecutions, and calamities. For when I am weak,
then I am strong
2 Corinthians 12:9 ESV

Each time you feel the void in any of its form you let God give you His grace for each moment.

Let us then with confidence draw near to the throne of grace, that we may receive mercy and find grace to help in time of need.
Hebrews 4:16. ESV

7. Empowered for His Glory

God has blessed us with two boys Demi and Dami. In Nigeria they attend a school that requires the students to wear school uniforms. Every day we ensure that their uniforms are well ironed, their shoes polished, and that they are well groomed. One of these days while I (Ade) was dressing them up, I noticed that they really did not care if their shoes were dusty or if their shirts were rumpled. Their dressing up neatly was more for us than for them. At their ages, it is the parents who get the glory for how neatly their children are dressed.

In the last part of the chapter on Your New Identity we considered the truth that we belong to God. Far more than we care that our boys are neatly dressed to school, God cares very much that we represent His true nature. It is God who gets the glory when we allow God to work out His plans in our lives. When we act in the love of God, in the wisdom of God, in the power of the Holy Spirit, the people around us see our good work and glorify our Heavenly Father.

For a long time I thought that only God gets the glory and we just enjoy the blessings, the fruit and the joy of working with God. However I have discovered that we also partake of the glory! Not that we receive credit for what God did, but we share in the joy and honor that is given to God because we are in Him and He in us. When a person becomes honored, those who work for him or with him share in the honor. His children also share in the honor. For example if you are a personal assistant to a man who becomes the president of a nation, you also begin to enjoy some respect and value simply through association with a man of honor. Similarly, the children of that man will be affected by the honor received by their dad.

Why has God empowered us so much? Why does He give all of Himself to us? It is because He loves us. Why should we let God receive all the Glory?

Because God is infinitely wiser than us, He is infinitely more powerful and He has a plan that is infinitely better than ours. If we allow Him to work out His plan, then He deserves to receive all the Glory.

When people see the progress in your life, when they see the joy that you have, the love that you give and receive, the miracles that you enjoy, they will want to know how you do it. It then becomes your responsibility and honor to let them know that it is the Lord God almighty that has done it in you.

What does this empowered life look like to God? It is simply a specimen of His great plan, great wisdom, and great power. Your life becomes a sample of what God can do with a willing heart. There is no limit for a man or woman who is totally yielded to the power of our Lord Jesus Christ. The apostle Paul says it like this:

" I can do all things through Christ who strengthens me".

Phi 4:13 NKJ

It is Christ that strengthens you! It is no longer your life but His. He must be the initiator, the sustainer and the completion of everything that concerns us. This does not mean that we spend countless hours in seclusion waiting for a "move of the spirit". There are times when we must go off to a secluded place to rejuvenate and receive fresh direction, especially after a season of much activity. However, the daily life of an empowered child of God is a life of constant dependence on the power of God. It is a life of constant attentiveness to the instructions of God! Those subtle directives of love that the Holy Spirit sends. You realize that without His wisdom, much time and resources will be wasted and much harm will be done.

What are some other practical steps to take?
1) Write down your life goals as you believe the Lord has placed in your heart! By life goal, I mean the top 3 things that you would like to do, to be, and

to contribute to this world before leaving it. Don't wait for a special voice from heaven. Simply write whatever comes to mind right now. Don't think about how it will be done, simply write with the understanding that you can do all things through Christ that strengthen you.

2) Write down all the changes that you need to make in your life in order to achieve the goals and vision you have written in step one above. If you need to learn some new skill write it down, if you need to buy some materials and get rid of some limiting attitudes, relationships or activities, write them down.

3) Think of all the people that you may need to help you on your way to fulfilling your God given vision. Write their names and think of ways you can connect with them. Make sure you write down a plan for achieving these connections. Do not permit yourself to say I don't know or I will do it later. What you write today may not work but the activity

of writing an option down, gives you the faith and the attentiveness to find a way.

4) Think of what you can do within the next 24 hours that will greatly contribute to achieving some of these goals. Write it down.

5) Locate a person who can help with these things you have written. Someone who believes in what God has deposited in you. Someone who has shown confidence in you in the past and continues to do so. Give them your list and ask them to be your mentor. Do it as soon as possible.

6) Do step four. Keep this list with you during your prayer times every day. Be ready to adjust it as God shows you a clearer picture.

7) Keep working hard at your life goals and enjoy the process. Choose not to worry that you are not sure of it. Just work hard at it as if you are sure and be very open to changing things if anything clearer

comes up. You are in for a great time. I can't wait to share your story with the rest of the world.

Other Tools

God has given us all that we need in the Bible. If you do not have a study Bible you will need to get one, a Bible concordance is also very good for reference. They will help lead you to answers that come up as you study more about your new identity.

There are so many other tools and resources that are very helpful. Many have asked me what I use during my time alone with God daily. And my response usually is, it varies. It depends a lot on what I am facing at the time. However, my Bible is the major part of my devotion. Usually, that is where I begin. Another vital part of my time with God is a note either in paper form or electronic form. I find that when I write down my thoughts I engage God's grace better. This way I am not just going through the motion of reading my Bible, I also write what I am getting from it down on paper. If you ever catch me praying or worshiping God, you will likely see me writing as well, most of the times I use my electronic device because of the easy access to whatever I write at any given time. But I find that using a notebook is by far better because you limit the distractions. This act of writing helps to allow God's words to cleanse my heart and I tend to see more results in my devotion.

Another thing that helps are books and songs from other great men and women of God (dead or alive). I use these based on topics I am studying per time. I cannot definitely state all the authors, ministers and music ministers that have blessed me, however these are a few of those that continue to make a mark in my life and in my walk.

Some of my favorite authors and ministers are:
Andrew Murray
A W Tozer
E. M Bounds
Charles Spurgeon
John & Stasi Eldredge
Joyce Meyer
Nancy Leigh Demoss

Watchman Nee

Some of my favorite music ministers are:

Don Moen

Darleen Czechs

Hillsong United

Kent Henry

Toby Mac

William McDowell

I love worshiping God in songs and many songs have brought my heart closer to my father, a few that I remember are listed here. The list is not exhaustive but gives a bit of information about my daily actions.

Additional Resources.

As God gives me His grace, I continue to work on developing resources that will help Christians both spiritually, financially, in their marriage/family and in their career.

Most of my resources are hosted on my websites:
www.adeandolu.com
www.olusobanjo.com
www.launchadream.com &
www.motivationalvideos.me

Each resource is designed to enrich your life as you become a person of influence and others will teach you how to turn some of your existing resources (your time, your skills, your habits, your hobbies, your experiences) into actual solutions for yourself and others.

My dream launcher's preliminary course: **Find Your First Profitable Idea** helps to identify an idea (from your time, your skills, your habits, your hobbies, your experiences) that you can turn into profit today. And another is my **Earn $1000 on the side** online course. (Both at www.launchadream.com)

Another resource I have is **From Yes To I Do** - A 13-week devotional for brides-to-be. Giving them vital advice they need as they plan their wedding and get ready to be married to the love of their lives. I created this in response to real (and relevant) questions I got from real brides to be over my years of counseling intending couples at Overcomers Assembly. (Found at www.adeandolu.com)

You may prayerfully look through to see what God would lead you into as you become more influential around people that God sent you to.

If you have any questions in any of the areas mentioned, don't hesitate to email me at olu@launchadream.com.

God bless you greatly.

Olu Sobanjo.

About the Authors

Olu (Oluwaseun) Sobanjo is passionate about Christ. Working alongside her husband, Ade she serves as co-pastor at Overcomers Assembly since its inception in 2005. Currently with 3 locations in Canada and a new plant in Kuje, Abuja, Nigeria; the Church continues to be home for ordinary people living extraordinary lives.

She is mother to two wonderful boys (Demi & Damilola). Olu is a mentor and inspiration to women everywhere. She loves to help and see people pursue a thriving life in Christ.

Her desire to meet the needs of women led her to start the ladies ministry (single and married) at her church. She hosts the Vessels of Gold Conference (an annual ladies conference) since 2007.

She worked in financial planning for about 5 years until she left her practice in July 2012 to devote herself to everything God has for her to do. She enjoys pursuing Christ daily. She loves doing business and teaching others to do the same.

Ademola (Ade) Sobanjo is the founding pastor of Overcomers Assembly in Canada. This church which started with his wife Oluwaseun as a prayer meeting in their living room in 2005 has since become a thriving church family with services in three different locations in Canada and one in Nigeria. He is passionate about discipleship and helping every believer fulfill their God giving potentials. Before obtaining his B.A in theology and going into fulltime pastoral ministry, Ade obtained a masters degree in Electrical Engineering and ran his own company in Montreal, Canada. He and Oluwaseun are blessed with two boys, Demi and Dami.

....

The principles in this book are intended to point your attention always to Jesus. For more information about

- Olu's seminars and conference schedule
- Engaging Olu as a speaker for your group
- Future books and materials
- Past and Current blog posts

Visit www.OluSobanjo.com

....

www.ingramcontent.com/pod-product-compliance
Lightning Source LLC
Chambersburg PA
CBHW032042040426
42449CB00007B/980